Give a Dog a Home

Also available
Give a Cat a Home

Give a Dog a Home

Dedicated to a little dog who joined
a family when they needed him most.

The original Scruffy Mutt and
inspiration for all that has come to be.

987654321
First published in 2008

Packaged by Susanna Geoghegan for
National Trust Books
10, Southcombe Street
London W14 0RA

An imprint of Anova Books Company Ltd

ISBN 978-1-906388-19-5

Little Dog Laughed Ltd
22a Parker Centre, Mansfield Road
Derby, DE21 4SZ
Tel: 01332 290605 Fax: 01332 290778
www.thelittledoglaughed.co.uk

Printed in China by Hung Hing

Introduction

Battersea Dogs & Cats Home was founded in 1860 by a courageous lady called Mary Tealby.

Being concerned by the large numbers of street dogs in London, she opened the Home in a stable yard in Holloway. In 1871 we moved to our present site in Battersea and started caring for cats in 1883. We now have three sites: at Battersea in south-west London, Old Windsor in Berkshire and Brands Hatch, Kent.

Since 1860 the Home has cared for over three million lost or abandoned dogs and cats. We aim never to turn away a dog or cat in need of our help and each year we take in over 12,000 of them. Many of the lost animals are reunited with their owners

within just a few days. Others require more intensive help
by our veterinary clinic or behaviour staff to help with their
individual problems and this means that their stay with us can
be a lot longer.

Battersea's staff and volunteers are some of the most
dedicated people you will ever meet. They go to extraordinary
lengths to help the animals, whether it is finding the perfect
new family or working home, fostering a dog or cat or hand-
rearing tiny kittens every four hours throughout the night.
They deal with the best and worst of situations with care,
compassion and feeling.

None of our work would be possible without the kindness and
generosity of our supporters. Battersea Dogs & Cats Home is
a registered charity and we rely totally on donations to fund
our work. This is one of the reasons that we were so delighted
to have the opportunity to collaborate with The Little Dog
Laughed. The funds raised from each book will directly help
the dogs and cats in our care and those yet to come to us.

It is wonderful to see in print the stories of our wonderful ex-residents, and especially to see how they have changed and touched the lives of their new owners.

On behalf of all the two and four-legged residents at the Home we would like to thank everyone at The Little Dog Laughed for choosing Battersea Dogs & Cats Home and especially Anna Danielle; her illustrations bring the dogs and cats to life. Thank you to the staff and owners who contributed their stories and their dogs and cats who sat patiently for their paw-traits!

And, of course, thank you for purchasing this book and for supporting Battersea Dogs & Cats Home.

The Rogan Family

Adopting one rescue dog is special; two is quite interesting; three is a talking point. Five is 'Oh my god, are all those dogs yours?'

Meet the Rogans and their beautiful girls.

They readily admit that life with five dogs is hectic to say the least, but they love every minute of it. The girls live, eat, sleep and play together, thoroughly enjoying their creature comforts. They know every inch of their local parks and particularly adore exploring the forest, running through the trees playing tag. In the winter months they visit the beach, piling into the family Mondeo. With the seats folded down the girls have the run of the back, causing much amusement to other road users.

At home, getting up to make a hot drink invariably means losing your seat, and the weekly shopping trolley always contains more food for dogs than humans.

Despite all the individual problems which led to the girls ending up in Battersea, the Rogans have experienced none of them. The only restriction they've faced is a lack of family holidays – however this pales in comparison to the unconditional love they receive five times over.

Each of the girls has her own individual character –

Chelsey is the timid one,

Kacey is their Little Miss Sensible,

Kiya is The Boss,

Molly is their hyperactive, loveable rogue,

and **Sandi** is their Little Old Lady.

This is how they all came to live under one roof.

Chelsey & Kacey

The Rogans' Battersea story began in the year 2000.

Following on from the loss of Lucy, their beloved faithful companion of fourteen years, the house felt horribly empty without canine company. So the search for a mongrel puppy began and after a successful interview, they adopted Chelsey, a puppy collie/shepherd cross.

Chelsey had been rescued from a home where the owner was seen mistreating the adult dogs. She settled in well but was extremely nervous of almost everything. As she was growing up so fast, the Rogans returned to Battersea for a new collar and advice on dealing with Chelsey's timid nature. The staff suggested adopting an older, more mature dog for Chelsey to follow and learn from.

Meet dog number two: our Kacey.

A beautiful, well-mannered mongrel, Kacey was about seven years old. She had been given to Battersea apparently for showing signs of aggression towards a toddler in her family.

So Chelsey met Kacey and they bonded immediately. Life was wonderful. They became firm friends and Chelsey, although still timid, started to come out of her shell.

A year later and as a birthday treat for Chelsey they went back to Battersea for new collars.

Kiya

So the Rogans headed over to Battersea
and purchased two lovely collars
for their special girls.

It seemed silly not to have a quick look round and that's when they spotted number three, Kiya.

A shy black and white lurcher type, roughly six months old, she had been gifted into Battersea because she chewed expensive trainers!

One look at Kiya and they melted.

Their minds started ticking over. What would it be like having three dogs? Could they cope? Would Battersea even allow them to adopt another? They plucked up the courage and asked the all-important question. The answer came back – yes – just so long as all the dogs got along together. So with a successful third interview under their collar, they took Kiya home to live with Chelsey and Kacey.

Life was even more fun with three dogs. It was just like having young children around. They played together, ate together and slept together. The inseparable trio.

Another happy year passed and before they knew it, it was again time for new collars, but that was definitely it – absolutely no more dogs!

Molly

Meet Molly, number four!

Sitting quietly at the front of her kennel was Dolly the Dalmatian. She was about six months old and very cute. Apparently deaf and a bit of a handful, she'd already had three homes. With her disability it was felt a multi-dog household would suit her best as she would be able to follow the other dogs and learn recall and training from them. So in for a penny, in for a pound! Dolly's name was changed to Molly and she joined the Rogans' household.

What a shock to the system! She was lovely, but sooooooooo hyperactive. Forget a bull, a Dalmatian in a china shop is far more destructive. Clumsy was an understatement. And greedy! Food left alone for a few seconds would instantly disappear down Molly's throat. One of the hardest parts was getting Molly to understand 'No' when she couldn't hear you.

The Rogans began to think they might have to admit defeat and send her back. They spoke in depth with Battersea's rehoming team and decided to give it another go: if they couldn't make it work Battersea would be sure to find her another good home.

So the Rogans persevered. They had Molly's hearing tested and she was actually only deaf in her left ear so all commands had to go to her right ear. It took a few months but they learnt from each other and Molly became a very loved and well-established member of the family.

Sandi

Life with four dogs? Well, they walk and run together, play tag together, eat together and sleep together.

They always want the toy the other dog has. They all want to greet you at once when you return home. The garden has been destroyed but life is absolutely wonderful!

Meet number five.

Sandi, a small Jack Russell cross, was sitting in a kennel looking very sorry for herself. She looked up at the Rogans with big brown eyes and they thought, 'You look cute' and then they walked on. And then they walked back!

She was about ten years old and a stray. After a fifth interview, Sandi went home to live with Chelsey, Kacey, Kiya and Molly. She settled in right away. It's possible she had lived with an elderly person because of her penchant for Polo mints and tea. She adores lying on the windowsill for hours on end watching the world go by.

So there you have it, the Rogan clan. A happier, more loving family you couldn't wish to meet.

Sadly, whilst this book was being written, Sandi was diagnosed with mammary cancer and underwent three operations. She responded well to treatment but then became ill again just before Christmas. The vet battled to save her but the cancer had spread to her stomach and lungs. Sandi's body language and eyes begged for release. The Rogans made the heartbreaking decision to let her go.

In loving memory of Sandi, deeply missed, but forever one of the family.

Mini

Mini, the Jack Russell, rides a Harley Davidson and is a bona fide member of two biking clubs, the Chillout Chapter and the Chiltern Hills Bike Club.

With over 22,000 miles under her belt, she has travelled the length and breadth of Britain and raised a great deal of money for Battersea along the way.

Mini's love for two wheels was discovered a week after Rob Oxley and Pat Nicklin adopted her. Somehow, she escaped and chased after Rob as he rode his bike down the drive. Slowing down, he scooped her up onto the petrol tank and she happily rode all the way back to the house. So Rob customised a leatherette tank cover, adapted a body harness and attached a short length of lead which secured Mini to the bike. Able to stand, sit or lie down, with hat and doggles on,

Mini took to the open roads. Winning hearts everywhere she goes, Mini is an extraordinary little dog. She is calm and gentle with no hint of the terrier temperament. Her picture has been taken thousands of times, even as she's doing 70mph on the motorway. Drivers slow down, unable to quite believe their eyes.

And fame has never gone to her head. At the HOG rally in Killarney she raised over £1000 in her little collecting tin by looking gorgeous and posing for photographs. Time is ticking on, but whilst her spirit is willing and the engine running, keep your eyes peeled for Mini, the chilled-out biker dog.

Tops

Faith and Alan Amos were first-time buyers, but instead of queueing at Ikea they headed straight to Battersea's Old Windsor site.

They knew that only a dog could make their new house a home. Immediately falling in love with Topic, a young chocolate brown Labrador, they discovered to their utter dismay he'd already found a home. Continuing their search but to no avail, they made to leave, very heavy hearted. A member of staff asked how they had got on. 'Well, there was one Labrador, but he's been sold.'

'Oh, if you mean Topic, I've just taken a call and his new home has fallen through.'

Hoorah for fate!

Ten years on, Tops has never looked back. He is everything you'd expect from a Labrador and more. Faith is a care nurse for the terminally ill and Tops often accompanies her to work. He has a real empathy with patients, unflinching even when patting gestures become quite violent with the patient's loss of motor skills.

He also has a remarkable memory. On a visit to the Wag and Bone show, a huge fundraising event, Tops became very agitated and began to pull and strain on his lead, seemingly intent on following a lady through the crowds. Thinking there was possibly chocolate on her shoe they finally caught up with the stranger and realised they all knew her. It was the lady who had sorted his adoption papers over eight years earlier. He simply wanted to say thank you!

Tarka

Some time later Faith and Alan were on the lookout for a companion for Topic.

They came across a litter of otterhound puppies that had been rescued from a bad breeder and Tarka was the last to be rehomed. Petrified and starving, they literally had to prise him away from the kennel wall. The emotional damage was severe and Tarka had obviously been the gentlest of the litter, losing out in the fight for the limited food on offer. The staff suggested an older dog might help with Tarka's rehabilitation and there could be none better for the job than Tops.

Falling in love with a dog with vacant eyes was very hard and the road to recovery was a long one. It was a whole year before Tarka waved his tail but they celebrated this monumental event with a party. The next milestone was being greeted when they returned home from work but it was a further three years before the true Tarka emerged, radiant, confident and energetic.

The dog who had no idea how to play now has his very own toy box and is making up for those lost puppy years. The dog who tried to blend into the corner now shares his basket and chews with his best friend who he simply adores. Topic's influence has also crept into Tarka's personality and he amuses other owners who can't believe his mellow, well-behaved character, so unlike otterhounds! At last, Tarka is finally happy in his own fur.

Doods

This was Dudley at sixteen, before Tricia had to make that awful, heartbreaking decision and have him put to sleep.

Struggling more and more, she simply couldn't let him suffer any longer.

A beloved dog and dearest companion, Dudley – Doods to his closest friends – had the most amazing life and accompanied Tricia on countless adventures. More than sixteen years ago she visited Battersea and a lively, boisterous dog of dubious heritage convinced her to take him home. It was one of the best decisions she ever made.

Dudley, an eight-month-old stray with origins unknown, was fully house trained. It's possible his previous owners couldn't cope with all his energy and by all accounts there was a lot of energy to cope with! He loved fell-walking in the Lake District and thoroughly enjoyed the benefits of a second home in Yorkshire with Tricia's parents. He would walk out with Tricia whenever she went horse riding and absolutely loved to travel: the train, underground, ferries and canal barges – nothing fazed him. Dudley even went up Ben Nevis in a cable car.

On a number of occasions, Tricia smuggled him into work and the boss never knew because he was so impeccably behaved.

Dudley had so much love to give and everyone who met him truly adored him. Perhaps when the pain of his loss eases and memories bring smiles and less sadness then Tricia will make her way back to Battersea and see who chooses her next.

Cracker & Jazz

Cracker and Jazz, the Jack Russell duo, assist Kate, one of Battersea's Driver Collection Officers.

At 6am they arrive at work and read through the list of dogs to be collected from various police stations, warden kennels and private veterinary clinics, all within the huge radius of the M25.

Cracker, a handsome smooth-haired chap, was eight weeks old when he was found locked in a hot car, dumped in a supermarket car park. Kate collected him from Forest Gate police station, a tiny bundle of fur tucked into the corner of a small cardboard box.

Jazz, a stray puppy, joined them a year later. She was placed on Kate's desk under the banner of 'friend for Cracker'. Originally smooth haired, she started to sprout wispy tufts giving her a distinct air of wisdom.

With the route decided, the trio head off into the joy of London commuter traffic. Cracker rests upon the dashboard, enjoying the warm air from the vents, whilst Jazz keeps a watchful eye for motorbikes and buses, barking whenever she sees one. She is very busy and very vocal for most of the journey. Sometimes their pick-ups include donated blankets and pet foods, all constantly in demand by the Home.

With their work done, they return to site around 1pm. They wait in the office whilst Kate debriefs the assessment team. Then it's time for home, a hearty meal and a well-deserved snooze before the start of another busy day.

Keano

Gill Raddings' company 'Stunt Dogs' has over twenty dogs on its books, including Wellard and Terrence from EastEnders.

With a BA honours from the British Institute of Dog Trainers, Gill provides dogs and many other animals for the film and television industry.

Gill has a close working relationship with Battersea and often adopts the bigger dogs that are difficult to rehome. Once she's assessed a dog, they'll spend on average three to four months in training. Gill has four dogs of her own, and her other adopted prodigies live with carefully vetted foster families. She takes full financial responsibility for each dog, providing their food and veterinary fees for life.

Away from the studio or film set, each dog leads a normal, loving family life. Regular exercise, tasty treats, lounging on the sofa: Gill imposes no restrictions on how they are homed just so long as they are loved and well cared for.

Training a dog for film and television is only possible if the dog actually wants to do it. Take Keano for example. Blessed with the highly sought-after looks of a scruffy mutt, he had the potential to be a great star. However, Keano has no interest in the world of luvvies and even less in being trained. He has had a few walk-on extra's parts but even that's asking a bit much. As far as Keano is concerned, acting is a mugs' game and he has better things to do with his time.

Blake

Blake, on the other hand, is the complete opposite to Keano.

A handsome but boisterous American bullmastiff cross, he was given to Battersea because his owners could no longer cope with him. A dog of his size and breeding takes very careful rehoming, so Battersea gave Gill a call.

Blake was incredibly strong and a real challenge on a lead. He adored hunting and when Gill adopted him it took all her strength and talent to get him under control.

His saving grace was his passion for training and Gill soon discovered that he was a complete natural in front of the camera. A tower of a dog, Blake exudes nobility and grace and has many acting credits to his name. It's hard to believe after seeing him on film and posing in the Fisher Price toy commercials that off camera he is an extremely excitable, happy, bouncing dog.

Blake has just completed a starring role in a German feature film entitled *Hardcover* that will certainly cement his fame in the fatherland. He has appeared in the television series *Silent Witness* and also has a part in the feature film *The Other Boleyn Girl*.

Blake's acting talents include walking backwards, playing dead, crawling on his stomach, holding an object, hiding his eyes and his particular favourite, walking with a limp. Who would have believed on that dark day, when he was given in to Battersea and his future seemed miserable and bleak, that life would turn out to be so much fun?

Bonnie

Bonnie's plight was captured on CCTV.

She had been thrown out of a car in the early hours of the morning onto the drive of Battersea's Old Windsor site. Just three months old, she was the most adorable bundle of fluff.

Gill spotted her and, although wary of taking on puppies, was bowled over by her confidence and strength of personality. Bonnie was born to act. Her particular forte is period dramas and she landed a major role in the BBC's costume drama *Cranford*. She was dressed in numerous outfits and completely doted on by Mrs Jamieson, a lethargic old widow with aristocratic connections, played by the actress Barbara Flynn. Bonnie mixed with a star-studded cast, including Dame Judi Dench, Imelda Staunton and Julia McKenzie. She is due to start

filming another period drama in the autumn in which Keira Knightley also has a starring role.

Bonnie is very used to mixing with great acting talent. She appeared alongside Johnny Depp in the film musical *Sweeney Todd* and discovered him to be most charming and approachable. She is also the face of the Harveys Furniture ads and finds modelling an interesting sideline to her acting career.

When Bonnie is not filming she lives a normal, happy life with four lively children and a Rottweiler called Klaus who incidentally has his own role in the BBC sitcom *Green Green Grass*. Bonnie's passion is her art and although the trappings of celebrity and fame are fun, walks, cuddles and mealtimes are far more precious.

Joshie

Meet Joshie the £20,000 terrier.

He limped into Battersea with a deformed paw and was diagnosed as a 'behavioural nightmare'. It took days to get a collar and lead on him and he seemed unrehomable.

However, Joshie had one thing going for him: Wendy, the Home's Fostering Co-ordinator. Away from the kennels, he was a different character and after a live-in assessment, Wendy adopted Joshie.

Unfortunately, it was nearly three months before he could go home: Joshie had a digit from his paw and his undropped testicles removed. He then developed kennel cough which was so severe that five years on he still sounds like a heavy smoker. Then after a dramatic loss of fur, he was tested for Cushing's Disease but the results were borderline. However, the diabetes test came back positive and treatment involved two insulin injections a day. After another bout of illness he had a second Cushing's test: again it was borderline but he'd contracted an *E. coli* infection that took nine months, an intravenous drip and four lots of antibiotics to cure. A third Cushing's test after Joshie went nearly bald came back positive.

Despite his ills, Joshie is a happy little dog and with help from his Jack Russell pal Teddy, he copes well with his recent blindness. He is the furry proof that insurance sometimes actually pays, and love knows no bounds.

Poppy

Poppy is an incredibly special Jack Russell who was given to Battersea because her owner could no longer afford to keep her.

Not only has she had a mammary tumour removed, but she is also totally blind, having contracted the eye disease glaucoma. She bravely endured two enucleation operations where they removed both eyeballs and sutured the eyelids shut. As traumatic as this sounds, it freed Poppy from excruciating pain and enabled her to start enjoying life again.

Samantha Jones first saw Poppy on the Battersea website and knew instantly that she was the perfect dog for her family. An affectionate, funny and gutsy little lady, Poppy has never let her blindness hold her back.

She is such a happy dog and loves running everywhere at great speed. She is full of confidence and bumping into objects doesn't worry her at all. She just bounces off and carries on her way. She adores squeaky toys and has endless fun chewing, chasing, and throwing them into the air. At times it's almost hard to believe she is blind. Poppy retains many of her facial expressions as her muscles still function normally and she often appears to be winking at you. She loves her food: the smell and taste of cod fillets make her drool and raw carrot sticks send her giddy with delight.

Disabled and blind dogs are often overlooked and remain unhomed, but the Joneses consider it a true privilege to be part of Poppy's life – their brave, inspirational little girl.

Harpur

Adopting a dog is about finding companionship, love – and exercise.

For Ben it was all those things plus a potential life-saver. A normal, sport-obsessed nine-year-old, Ben suddenly developed rashes on his body and complained of feeling tired. He became seriously ill and was diagnosed with a very rare autoimmune disease. Juvenile dermatomyositis attacks the skin and muscles and can go on to the internal organs. Although there is no known cure, with drugs and keeping fit it can be contained and even go into remission.

Ben desperately wanted a dog, and with exercise now so important, the family headed off to Battersea.

Harpur, a shy greyhound/lurcher had been found wandering on Iver golf course. Ben spotted him and knew he was the one.

Mum, however, was not so sure: Harpur was quite big, so they kept looking. Five return visits with various family members in tow and Ben was still adamant that Harpur was the one. During their adoption interview they were amazed to discover that only one dog matched their profile. Ben was right: Harpur was the one.

Ben's condition made getting out of bed unaided and using the stairs very difficult. Having Harpur downstairs gave him the motivation and will to get better, and having Ben's love helped Harpur overcome his shyness and gain confidence.

Hopefully with Harpur in his life and his loving family by his side, Ben will find the courage and determination to battle on.

Lyla

Nicky and Julian Richardson were the first couple not employed by Battersea to become foster carers.

Was it successful? Well sort of. They kept the dog and Nicky gave up her job and joined the Battersea payroll!

After they'd responded to a foster carers' ad in the local paper they were visited by Battersea's rehoming team and attended seminars on responsible dog ownership and basic training. Then they met Lyla and knew immediately she was the sort of dog they would have chosen for themselves. She was an extremely nervous, young, pretty collie cross with black fur. Her past is unknown but she had obviously been on the streets for quite a while to be so thin.

Lyla was also suffering from demodectic mange and had bald patches on her neck, nose and legs. In the beginning she hid under the bed or behind the sofa but gradually she grew braver. Lyla's first walk on Wimbledon Common was truly heartwarming as she ran through the grass with the biggest grin on her face. Her fur started to grow back thick and luscious; she put on weight and wagged her tail constantly.

Lyla was now ready for adoption but the Richardsons just couldn't part with her. They knew they had failed as foster carers but whilst helping Lyla grow from a scared, skinny mutt into a confident, happy dog they had fallen completely in love.

Boss

Dedicating their lives to fighting crime, Battersea rescue dogs Boss and Harvey work alongside their handler PC 591A Lucas in the constant battle to make London a safer place.

Boss the German shepherd was found as a stray and swiftly assessed by Battersea's Working Dog Specialist as having the potential to join the police force. Intelligent, active and quick to learn, Boss was readily accepted onto the training course. After an intensive twelve weeks Boss passed with flying colours and gained his licence to become a General Purpose Police Dog for the City of London Police.

His duties include maintaining public order through crowd control: sometimes his presence is deterrent enough. He is fully licensed to chase, detain and locate hidden suspects.

On a recent night duty Boss was involved with a successful search for a suspected burglar. Two suspects had been apprehended by police but a third got away and was believed to be somewhere in the nearby park. In complete darkness, Boss located the hidden suspect in the play area, squashed into a children's playhouse. His talents also include finding discarded property such as knives or guns; his keen sense of smell is invaluable when searching for vital evidence.

Boss loves his job; it helps keep his active mind stimulated. Add in the regular exercise, healthy meals, daily grooming and the chance to take down the bad guys, and you have one very contented dog.

Harvey

Harvey the springer/cocker spaniel cross is a Specialist Search Dog, proactive in finding currency, firearms and drugs.

Originally given in to Battersea when his owners couldn't cope with his dominant personality, Harvey was a clear candidate for the police force with his intelligence, drive and natural instinct to 'seek and search'.

Canines play an amazing role in modern-day policing: they save precious search time and help pinpoint specific areas that aren't obvious to the human eye.

Harvey's exceptional strike rate includes assisting in a raid on a crack house in North London. Police officers had cleared the building and two people were detained. Harvey swiftly searched each room until he locked onto a strong scent; he then assumed a static freeze, pressing his nose up against his find. It was a loaded hand gun hidden inside a vacuum cleaner.

He has found crack cocaine hidden in a baby's pushchair and large amounts of currency. With vehicle searches, Harvey's phenomenal sense of smell gives officers the upper hand. Without Harvey it's possible they might not have searched the airbag that had been deflated or the area between the roof and lining or even behind the lights. The strength of Harvey's reaction helps officers decide whether a suspect's explanation is fact or fiction.

The relationship between Battersea and the police force is a healthy one; the dog's welfare always paramount for both. Harvey and PC Lucas are more than happy to testify to that.

Flossie

Arriving at Battersea is a pivotal moment for many.

Flossie is no exception. Found on the streets, starved and extremely ill, she spent a month in Battersea's veterinary clinic. Her second piece of good fortune was being adopted by Celia Barnett.

Celia is a researcher in the art department of a film company, working for the Production Designer on big feature films. Flossie has exclusive access to the filming of *Harry Potter* and *James Bond* and meets many famous people. However, she abides by a strict code of secrecy and no amount of her favourite sardines would tempt her to an indiscretion.

Every day is varied – sometimes she visits the studios at Shepperton or Pinewood, but her favourite is Leavesden. There are lots of strange buildings to explore; huge tree trunks which you can't dig under and doors that don't go anywhere. Flossie adores the hustle of studio traffic – smoke machines, costume rails, big lights and trailers.

The best part of Flossie's day is lunch. She is a natural sprinter and shows off her speed with her work colleagues, the King Charles from Drapes, a Jack Russell from Production, the beagles from Special FX, a Staffie and greyhound from the Creature Shop and Sam, the producer's puggle.

Life had been pretty grim for Flossie but it is delightful to see her so happy, and to see the big smiles she receives from everyone she meets.

Henry the Wonder Dog

Henry the Wonder Dog was dramatically saved from a burning building by firemen.

Sadly his owners were untraceable after the fire. Clearly injured, he was seen immediately by a Battersea vet who found that his front leg was so badly broken it couldn't be saved. After amputation he was transferred to the Old Windsor site to recuperate, giving him time to build up his confidence on three legs.

When Dave, Margery and their young daughter Gemma went to the Home they spotted by lovely Jack Russell cross. Standing in a kennel wagging his tail, they could only partly see him. They asked to meet him and were surprised when the dogs' home attendant said, 'Oh, the three-legged one.'

As Margery and Gemma dealt with the paperwork, Dave watched a small girl come up and pat him. Another dog came over to inspect. Henry didn't even growl: that was good enough for Dave and Henry was on his way home.

Henry has a petmobile but much prefers riding in a large shopping bag, especially if Dave takes him up to the pub. He has attended folk festivals and been boating on the River Exe in Devon. He walks in Windsor Great Park and he is a total babe magnet – attractive ladies find him irresistible.

Recently Henry started losing weight and was diagnosed with the cancer Cushing's Disease. With medication he's holding his own and the family take comfort in the many happy moments they've all had since he entered their lives.

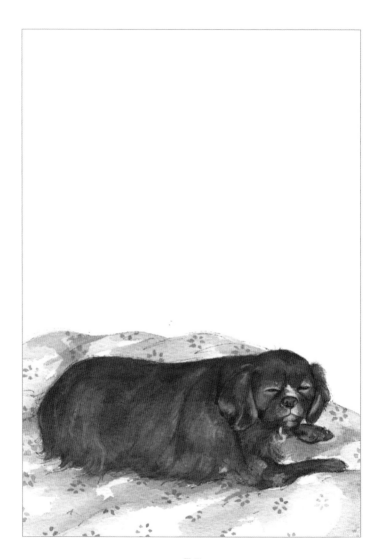

Dudley

Despite being clinically obese, totally furless, resembling a little pig and smelling really quite bad, Dudley was adopted within twenty-four hours.

Sam O'Connor, Head of Rehoming at the Old Windsor site took one look at this funny little dog and knew he was meant to be part of her life.

So began the long journey back to fitness. Dudley was terribly lethargic and so overweight he could barely walk. It was months before he managed a stroll around the block. As his fur began to grow back, Sam discovered she had an orange Cavalier King Charles Spaniel with a funny, zesty little personality.

Initially, Dudley had been diagnosed with a hypothyroid problem which partly explained his obesity. He then received a second health blow. Muffled by the thick wall of fat surrounding his heart, it wasn't until he started to shed the pounds that the vets discovered he had the beginnings of heart failure. Added to all this was his loss of hearing, the result of a chronic ear infection caused by too much skin closing the ear drum.

However, none of this has dampened his love of life and he thoroughly enjoys his days working in the office and watching the comings and goings at the Windsor site. He and his great pal Tia have positioned their baskets in front of the huge ceiling-high windows and pride themselves on the fact that very little escapes their attention.

Tia

Tia is Dudley's best friend.

She is also a big television star, or at least she will be when she finally gets that all-elusive big break. A young Border terrier cross with a beautiful little face, Tia is a natural performer.

She was given in to Battersea because her family couldn't cope with two puppies. Tia displayed nervous aggression and had been badly attacked by another dog. She had not been socialised as a puppy and had a penchant for chasing joggers and cyclists.

Tia needed her energy channelling into something positive and realising her love for the camera and a tendency towards the theatrical, Sam saw her potential immediately. Tia is a fast learner and with hard work and patience Sam has broadened Tia's skills base to include a whole repertoire of tricks. She can look to the right, wave, high five, walk backwards, sneeze, spin in both directions, reverse around legs, touch with her nose and paw, take a bow, play dead, walk on hind legs, bounce on the spot, open a book and close a door to name but a few.

Whilst waiting to be discovered Tia keeps up her day job in the offices at Old Windsor. She is one of the official 'meeters and greeters' on site and excels in her role as mascot for the home, posing for any publicity shots that are required. She is also the ears for her deaf friend Dudley and ensures he doesn't miss out on any potential fun.

Treacle & Honey

Paul and Nicki Clements are Dog Wardens for Runnymede Council and as such have a close working relationship with Battersea's Old Windsor site.

With Rosie the Border collie, Pickles the Jack Russell, three cats – Derek, Graham and LP – plus three horses you'd assume there wasn't much room for anyone else.

Treacle, a two-year-old black Labrador, was found on the streets in Sutton. Grossly overweight, it's believed she was rarely exercised and that encouraged her escape artist tendencies. At first they had to keep her fenced in but the little wanderer soon started to lose weight with a regulated diet and proper exercise. In a short space of time Treacle had settled happily into the family routine with all thoughts of escape banished to the past.

Then at Christmas 2006, Battersea asked the Clements if they would foster Honey the yellow Labrador over the holiday period. The kennel environment can be extremely distressing for some dogs and it's beneficial for the animal to have time out. The Clements felt confident fostering Honey as neither were particularly keen on yellow Labs. However, Honey had other ideas and fell head over heels for Paul. By the end of the Christmas break it was clear to all that Honey would not be going back to Battersea.

Since then Treacle and Honey have become inseparable: the Hinge and Bracket of the dog world.

Big Henry

Then along came Henry. A massive seventy kilos of yellow Labrador.

The Battersea staff see and deal with abuse and neglect in many different guises. Henry had previously been adopted by a lady who over a period of three years let him get bigger and bigger until she returned him to Battersea no longer able to cope with his size. A quick call to Paul, and Henry was on his way to the Clements' household for fostering, dieting, exercise and rehabilitation.

Henry was clinically obese, indeed he was so large he couldn't even move his neck. Obviously he struggled to walk and playful tussle with other dogs was unthinkable. He was unable to take more than four steps at a time and even wagging his tail was an effort.

A sad aspect of this tale is that Henry never once showed signs of greediness or begged for food.

Paul and Nicki worked their magic and as the weight came off a new dog emerged. The more pounds Henry shed the happier he became and at the end of five months they had a very sociable, happy dog with an extremely playful character. He absolutely adores games and loves being part of the Clements' menagerie.

The vets at the Old Windsor site have given Henry the all-clear and he is now available for adoption, desperately hoping for better luck third time round.

Bruno

It's 7.30am and Bruno has just been collected from Norbury Police Station.

He had been found tied to barbed wire fencing on open wasteland. He is loud, aggressive and malnourished. Life has not been good for this Staffie cross.

Bruno has never been a member of the family; he's never even been a dog. In his owner's eyes he is mere 'blingage', the latest trend on the street. Left alone for hours, rarely walked or socialised, he is a victim of the drug and gang culture, used as a threatening status symbol. From a pup he has been kicked and goaded into attack.

Once the inevitable has occurred, the dog is dumped, the owners unable to control what they have created. These ignorant people take a happy, fun-loving breed that make great family pets and turn them into antisocial fighting machines, reinforcing a stereotype that completely maligns the breed.

Bruno will be assessed for seven days by Battersea's Behaviour Unit who will try their best to turn him into a happy, sociable dog ready for a new home. Unfortunately, his story is all too common and his breed equate to one-third of the dogs coming into Battersea.

In the majority of cases the psychological damage is too severe and Battersea are left to pick up the pieces. It is a very sad and depressing situation for a charity based on compassion, love and goodwill to spend more and more of its time dealing with society's irresponsible trends.

Petal

Stray Petal arrived at Battersea looking more like a small grey, wrinkled elephant than a Westie.

She was totally bald and her legs bled from the slightest touch. She smelt awful and was a very pitiful sight. Lots of TLC from the Battersea staff and a kind donation of Eight Hour Cream from Elizabeth Arden helped Petal's healing process.

Within weeks her fur began to grow and her 'little madam' character blossomed. She chewed through numerous leads and soon gained top dog status in the fundraising office. And then there was more good news: a potential new home, with a florist! Samantha Sprigg and her son Tom had been considering adopting a dog for quite some time. On seeing Petal the decision was instant.

However, managing Petal's skin condition has taken a great deal of time and care with evening primrose oil in her meals and cream rubbed into her chest and paws daily. Continuous courses of antibiotics and spotting the early warning signs for a flare-up have all been part of the learning process.

Petal's working day starts with her daily walk through Petworth Park. Once at work, she settles down on her comfy bed for a mid-morning snooze. After lunch she explores the shop and soaks up the compliments from her adoring customers. Tom takes care of her entertainment needs and there is even romance in the air – a dashing Maltese terrier/Jack Russell cross called Percy whom Petal simply adores. Yes, life is indeed blooming marvellous!

Poppy

Meet Poppy, the semi-finalist of 'Britain's Top Dog' and a member of Battersea's fundraising team.

A Staffie cross, she was given to the Home when her owners got divorced. Suffering severe demodectic mange, a skin condition often caused by overbreeding and stress, she looked like an adult dog with bald patches around her feet and mouth.

Michelle, Battersea's Events Officer, has a soft spot for Staffies. She had sat with Poppy on her arrival and was dismayed to find she was still with the Home four months later. Her condition wasn't improving: Poppy desperately needed a break from kennels. Having fostered over twenty-five dogs, Michelle took Poppy home. By treating her skin with natural remedies and monitoring her diet, Poppy soon flourished. As did Michelle's soft spot,

and the adoption papers were quickly signed.

Poppy's working week varies. One day could be spent assisting the Education Officer on a school visit, talking about Battersea and responsible dog ownership. Another could be spent preparing for fundraising events like Crufts and Discover Dogs. She excels in her ambassadorial role for the Home and her breed.

However, it's not all hard work for this kind-natured canine. Squirrel chasing is a park highlight and Poppy amongst the pigeons has her smiling from ear to ear. A breed with a bad reputation, Poppy is the complete opposite to the Staffie stereotype and living proof that you should always judge the owner before the dog.

Louie

It was a cold, damp October morning when Mark Prior visited Battersea's Old Windsor site.

In a kennel was a Belgian shepherd cross, a little old fella affectionately named 'Spoons'. He was not coping well in kennels, and was painfully thin and dishevelled; he was also suffering from a tiresome stomach upset. Despite this, Mark knew at once he'd be taking him home.

Spoons was renamed Louie and he was soon devoted to Mark, always ready to greet him with his biggest smiley face. Louie was not a young dog, possibly seven, but he had bundles of energy and loved affection and cuddles, giving far more than he ever received. He was an amazing guard dog; very rarely did mail make it past the tooth stamp of Louie the 'canine franking machine'.

For nine glorious years they shared the same home until on the 4th of December 2007 Louie fell asleep for the last time. His frail back legs had succumbed to the inevitable ageing process and coupled with some mal-aligned discs in his lower back had left him unable to sit, stand or get up without obvious discomfort.

Mark wasn't prepared for just how much he missed Louie, his lovely dear old friend.

Dogs of a certain age often get overlooked or bypassed for the younger puppy. An older dog has just as much love and devotion to offer, so don't discount a face with a little grey round the muzzle, for, as with humans, life experience can be a very good thing.

Red

Battersea staff were completely baffled when over a space of three weeks they entered the kennel area to discover a number of dogs roaming loose and the kitchens raided.

A practical joker? Except all the doors were bolted with no sign of a break-in. The ghost of Mary Tealby, founder of the Home? No! But what if …

The mystery needed solving before Battersea was swamped with wannabe Ghostbusters. CCTV was installed and when the tapes were played back they discovered it was an inside job. The culprit? Red the lurcher!

A malnourished stray, Red had been at Battersea for four months before revealing his Houdini talents. Using his teeth and paws Red pulled back the bolt on his door and set himself free. Red obviously decided that eating alone was no fun and unbolted the doors for his favourite pals.

Amusingly, Red consistently left the rather yappy Jack Russell in solitary confinement. The band of brothers then tucked into their midnight feast of dog biscuits.

Red's escapades hit the headlines across the world and Battersea received over 400 calls offering him a new home. The cheeky, handsome lurcher enjoyed his fifteen minutes of fame and the extra media attention brought additional offers of homes for all his 'break-out buddies'.

Being a sociable character Red finally chose a family with three other dogs and now avoids the limelight. He's got what he wanted and although the fame was fun, nothing beats real love and a good home.

Hamlet

You can take the dog out of Japan but can you take Japan out of the dog?

Hamlet came from a rescue centre in Kansai where for more than five years he'd existed in an open field, often hunting his own food. A painfully withdrawn, timid dog with a soulful expression, Hamlet arrived from Japan in an attempt to raise awareness of the plight of many dogs in that country. Pedigree toy breeds generally have an exceptionally good life. However, larger mongrel breeds in rural areas do not fare so well.

Marika, a receptionist at Battersea's Old Windsor site, and coincidentally also Japanese, immediately offered to adopt him.

Having never lived in a house, Hamlet spent months desperately trying to get out. When he wasn't eating the curtains or planning his escape he'd sleep for hours on end. His lack of socialisation had left him devoid of normal doggy emotions: no tail wagging or barking, and even his sleep looked uncomfortable. For Marika it was like sharing her home with a quiet lodger, occasionally bumping into each other in the kitchen.

It has taken a great deal of patience, love and care to build Hamlet's confidence and he is slowly beginning to respond. He is now bilingual and helps on reception during the day, and his favourite evenings are spent snuggling up on the sofa next to Marika watching the soaps. He still maintains a certain distance that may never leave him but life is definitely on the up.

Cass

Gillian English has owned dogs all her life.

Growing up as a young girl in Chelsea, all her family dogs came from Battersea. When her dearly beloved Sebastian, a yellow Labrador and quite possibly the 'bestest dog in the whole wide world ever' passed away she was desolate. He'd been with them since she got married and she couldn't even contemplate owning another dog.

She lasted seven months before admitting her immaculately clean house felt lonely. Having had Sebastian from a puppy she was more inclined to adopt an older dog and after visiting Battersea she came away with two kennel mates, Arthur and Cass.

Cass was a ten-month-old whippet cross who had come in off the streets. Gillian believes he may have been thrown from a vehicle because whenever he saw a van he'd start shaking, wet himself and be sick. Completely neurotic, Cass barked at the slightest noise and enjoyed being high maintenance all his life.

Cass and Arthur were great friends and constantly got into mischief. Shortly after adopting them, Gillian came home to find her daughter's Christmas present from her grandmother, a rabbit fur coat, shredded into little pieces and two dogs playing tug of war with the sleeves. On one occasion Cass was attacked by another dog and lumbering Arthur leapt into action to defend his friend, earning himself the nickname Danger Dog.

Cass reached the grand age of sixteen and is remembered fondly for being a very loveable pain.

Arthur

Arthur, a seven-year-old black Labrador cross, had obviously been mistreated in his previous life.

Raising your hand even slightly caused him to cower and shake and he'd also been starved. As time passed he conquered his fears but the need for food never dissipated. Arthur's sole aim in life was to eat.

His true food passion was cake, the best discovery in the world.

One Christmas, Arthur kept disappearing from the lounge: not so unusual in itself, but then he was sick all over the kitchen floor. When Gillian went to get the beautifully decorated Christmas cake from the dining room she discovered he'd polished off the lot.

His second cake misdemeanour was on her daughter Rebecca's fifteenth birthday. Rebecca had a fantastic tennis court sponge cake,

with net, umpire and players. Arthur tucked into his share and very kindly left a little corner for the rest of the family to enjoy.

On another occasion Arthur went missing whilst on a walk. Gillian searched everywhere but with little success. Then she received a call from Banstead Golf Club informing her that Arthur was in the kitchen and had helped himself to two pints of beer and five packets of crisps!

In his latter years, Arthur went blind and deaf but still enjoyed his walks. The golf course is part public land and if he wandered off, nine times out of ten Gillian would find him attached to an unsuspecting golfer, nose in groin.

A legendary dog, Arthur will never be forgotten.

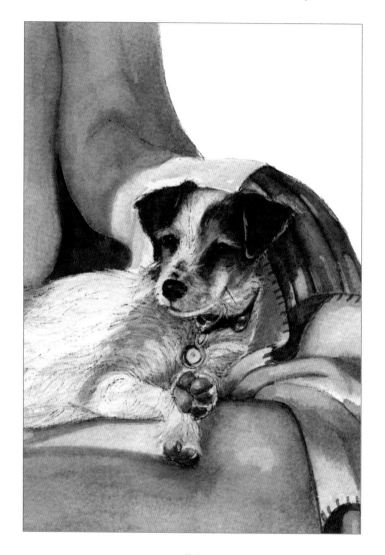

Charley Farley

Puppy Farley was found in the gutter huddled next to the body of his dead emaciated sister.

Almost furless, covered in mange, smelling terrible, he was literally hours away from death. He was taken to Battersea's Old Windsor site where he received round-the-clock attention. His chance of survival was 50/50.

Thankfully, the odds went in his favour and he began to show signs of improvement. Each day that passed saw Farley getting stronger. He was fostered by retired couple Mick and Jean O'Neil who regularly foster animals that need special attention or a break from kennels. Mick jokes that it keeps them active and is far cheaper than joining a gym. They continued aiding Farley's recovery with medicated baths and lots of cuddles.

Amazingly, Farley showed no signs of trauma. Like most puppies, he was into everything, running everywhere at great speed and pouncing on unsuspecting soft toys.

Finally, Farley was well enough for adoption. Unable to adopt Amber the beautiful lurcher because she was too strong for them, the Bannisters were introduced to Farley and that was that. Farley was off to start a new life in Devon.

Due to his comic nature he was soon renamed Charley Farley after the Ronnie Corbett character. Every day he has a manic moment tearing around the bungalow and is a constant source of amusement in his agility class. Long walks on the beach and chasing seagulls are his idea of pure heaven.

India & Marvin

India, the German shepherd, and Marvin, the Rottweiler, are both rescues, India from Old Windsor and Marvin from Battersea.

India has a sweet, calming nature and is a great mentor for Marvin.

Marvin had been found by a policeman dumped in a supermarket car park. Less than three months old, he earned the Battersea nickname Starvin' Marvin because he was so hungry. It took quite a while for staff to allay his 'next meal' fear.

Paul and Gillian Stribling saw Marvin on Battersea's website and couldn't resist a quick visit. They later returned home with Marvin who settled in immediately. A very bright boy, he definitely knows which side his bread is buttered on. Marvin is enjoying himself immensely in his new home. He works very hard taking various 'essentials' to the garden: Paul's boots, Gillian's washing-up gloves, full lemonade bottles, guests' shoes. Size is not an issue – he somehow manages to manoeuvre himself and the object through the dog flap.

A very comical pair, India and Marvin are both addicted to watching television, sitting relaxed on the sofa. All Marvin needs is a pipe and India, the best china. Marvin has also been helping Gillian with the garden. He has very nearly finished his 'Big Hole to Australia' project which Gillian is thrilled about!

After a terrible start in life, India and Marvin are thoroughly enjoying being loved, cuddled and spoilt rotten. Life is very good in the Stribling household.

Poppy

Prone to some classic 'I want to be alone' moments, Poppy is the Greta Garbo of the dog world.

With her expressive eyes, Chihuahua-sized body and German shepherd fur coat, Poppy is unique and knows it.

She was found as a stray, wandering the streets of London, but due to her nervous nature and a very bad case of kennel cough, she was transferred from Battersea to the Old Windsor site for a swifter recovery aided by the peaceful country setting of the Home.

Sharon Evans was working for an IT company when she adopted Poppy and under her love and care Poppy's true nature quickly emerged. Four years later she was back at Old Windsor: not as a rescue case, but as an official 'meeter and greeter'. Sharon landed her dream job working for the Home and Poppy excelled in her new self-appointed role, always putting on her very best face when amongst her public.

The lunchtime walks which can sometimes consist of seven or even eight dogs are a particular favourite although Poppy would never admit it. She has always retained an aloof distance from other dogs, and yet, secretly, she thoroughly enjoys being part of the pack.

Poppy is also a bit of a couch potato, although she argues that certain activities are simply below a dog of her breeding. She is happy to chase, frolic and dance when she's in the park but wasting precious energy walking there when one can be carried is plain ridiculous.

Rhea

Veterinary nurse Lyn O'Byrne was devastated when her two beautiful lurchers were stolen from work.

There had been a spate of dog thefts in the area, the culprits stealing the dogs to sell or work.

Lyn believes they were probably after Leggit, the bigger, stronger lurcher, who thankfully lived up to his name and escaped back to Lyn. Sweet little Rhea was not so fortunate and being a happy, trusting soul it's quite probable she didn't realise she'd been stolen.

Lyn did everything she could think of to find her, putting up 'missing' posters in local vets, fly-leafleting her area and searching open wasteland. It took four years before Lyn finally admitted defeat and gave up all hope of ever seeing Rhea again. She adopted a greyhound called Taz who joined Leggit and Kayleigh,

a lurcher/terrier cross Lyn's boss had insisted she rescue!

During Rhea's absence Lyn had moved from Kent to West Yorkshire and remembered to notify Petlog, managers of the microchip database, of her new address. It was thanks to this that Battersea were able to contact Lyn and tell her the extraordinary news: Rhea had been found in Kent and brought into the Home, nearly seven years after being stolen.

Lyn raced down to Battersea for a grand reunion but is not convinced Rhea remembered her. However, Leggit was a different matter: Rhea was ecstatic to see him, following him everywhere, and quickly settled down as if she'd never been away.

Humphrey

Nicola and Glenn Sutcliffe adopted Humphrey by accident.

They thought the description of Humphrey on the card matched that of a cute, lively Jack Russell. When the kennelhand brought Humphrey out, he was a completely different dog. A 'Battersea Allsorts', Humphrey was a mix of terrier, corgi and dachshund. Thin and frightened, he rolled onto his back and gave a snarl, but it was bravado. He obviously needed a lot of love and attention. So Nicola and Glenn took Humphrey home.

It wasn't easy. Humphrey had clearly been mistreated and had psychological problems, but over the years he grew to love them both and eventually all his behavioural problems vanished.

The day Humphrey left Battersea was the same day the Foot and Mouth outbreak began. He couldn't go for walks so the Sutcliffes took him to the Isles of Scilly for his first holiday.

Humph went on every family holiday after that, covering most of Britain. He walked the south-west coastal paths and even tried to drive the campervan when they toured Scotland.

Sadly, Humphrey developed arthritis and then lost his sight and hearing, but he was a remarkable dog and never gave up trying. On a visit to Nicola's mother's house, Humphrey had a stroke and they made the heartbreaking but humane decision to end his suffering.

Free from pain, rest in peace dearest Humph.

Crista

Whilst watching the BBC's live broadcast from Battersea Dogs & Cats Home, David Sturgess was instantly drawn to the plight of Crista the Japanese Akita.

Having recently lost his dear friend and companion Thor, also an Akita, David had no intention of getting another dog. Thor was irreplaceable.

However, Crista's story touched his heart and he emailed Battersea expressing his interest. Akitas are beautiful dogs, but with a dominant nature they are not a breed suitable for everyone.

Crista had been found seriously injured beside a railway line. Passers-by had seen her but it was two days before someone reported it. She was so badly injured that she had to have a complete amputation of her left foreleg. Despite all the publicity, no attempt was made to claim her. After a telephone interview,

Crista went to David's home on a trial basis. He had worried about how Crista would cope with the stairs up to his house but she bounced up them with ease. Neither needed a week to decide and the papers were signed.

Crista's new home is in the country, it's very hilly and provides great therapy for her. Having developed extra muscles to compensate for the missing leg, she can run, jump and chase rabbits as well as the next dog. Crista is a very loyal, spirited dog and is good company. Thor's place in David's heart will never diminish but providing Crista with a loving home and seeing her happy brings enormous satisfaction.

Harry

Battersea's Chief Executive, Jan Barlow, took Harry the spaniel home on a Friday to help with the shortage of kennel space.

Hopefully, over the weekend, a kennel would become available and Harry would be up for adoption. By Monday, Charlie, Jan's golden retriever, had fallen head over heels for Harry and so had Jan. Harry was staying!

Harry was given in to the Home because his previous owners couldn't cope with his energy. He is incredibly bright and Jan realised he was from working gundog stock. In an enclosed garden he is relaxed, but when free his thoughts are totally consumed by game birds and rabbits.

Seeing that Harry needed more, Jan enrolled him in Mullenscote Gundog School. They had trained a number of Battersea dogs and Harry thrived, adoring the mental stimulation and the chance to respond to his natural instincts.

Harry also helped save Charlie's life. Charlie developed lumps on his face. A veterinary diagnosis felt it was nothing to worry about but Harry clearly wasn't convinced. He wouldn't leave Charlie alone, consistently focusing on one particular lump; he kept licking and pawing at it until the lump became infected. After a course of antibiotics failed to heal the problem, Jan insisted the lump was removed. When the biopsy results came back, it was identified as a 'mast cell tumour', one of the most aggressive forms of cancer. Without removal, it would have spread and killed Charlie. Those overcrowded kennels were a life-changing blessing for them all.

MissyChief

MissyChief's nickname is born from
the mischievous twinkle in her eye
and her sheer exuberant love of life.

She always has a smile on her face and her happiness and joy for living are completely infectious.

Missy is a feisty, long-legged, rough-coated Jack Russell with ears to die for. She spent over two years at Battersea waiting for Pat and Paul Elliot to come and find her. They had been grieving for the loss of their first dog, Spotty. She had been a rescue dog and in her memory they wanted to rehome another.

Missy was the total opposite in looks but as she gently took the treat from their hands, in exactly the same manner as Spotty, the decision was instant.

Nothing escapes Missy's attention. She is so inquisitive and watches the Elliots' exploits with utter fascination. A recent hedge-trimming task was closely observed by Missy and for fun they cut a little cubby hole into the foliage for her. Missy leapt straight in, turning around with a grin that stretched from ear to ear. She regularly attends agility classes and always steals the show. The Elliots dutifully provided her with hurdles at home and all the while she practises she wears her trademark smile.

The fun and joy in her life spills over into all those around her and while it saddens the Elliots to think of MissyChief's long stay at Battersea, they thank their lucky stars she waited for them.

Sensor

When Estelle Lloyd Thomas answered a phone call from Battersea on Christmas Day it was the best present she had ever received.

Three weeks prior to the call the Thomases had been burgled. Sensor, the Dalmatian and Lucy, the Jack Russell slept in the stables and had been put to bed for the night. Halfway through their evening meal the Thomases turned with surprise to see Lucy jumping up and down at the French doors, barking madly. The stables had been stripped of horse tack; Lucy had escaped but Sensor was gone. All calls to the police, rescue centres and veterinary practices proved fruitless, and the family was devastated.

However, the day before Christmas Eve, Battersea's Old Windsor site received Sensor, and thankfully she was microchipped.

A lady had bought her from a man in a pub after taking pity on her look of misery. However she had given her to the Home the next day believing she wasn't house trained. So on Boxing Day morning, Estelle, her husband, her mother and her daughter all made the journey to Old Windsor to collect Sensor. It was an emotional moment but there was still a seven-hour journey back along the traffic-jammed M25 before Sensor finally made it home. Everyone was exhausted but glad to have Sensor back – and none more so than Lucy. With new beds in the conservatory for both dogs, Sensor soon recovered from her ordeal, became a proud mum and put those dark days firmly behind her.

Charlie

A cheeky little charmer, Charlie's experience of being tied up near London City Airport has left little sign of emotional damage.

The only clue to his traumatic start in life is his avid fascination for plane spotting!

A true scruffy mutt, Charlie has oodles of character and a 'butter wouldn't melt' expression. Liz McWalter, Battersea's Senior Intake and Assessing Co-ordinator, applied for adoption and soon discovered that the look was a bluff and that he has an uncanny knack of getting exactly what he wants.

A typical working day starts with an early morning train ride where Charlie casts his magic and before reaching Waterloo has usually secured a commuter's comfortable lap. He always stops for a chat at the coffee stall on Queenstown Road then it's into work for breakfast and a mid-morning snooze on the sofa.

Lunchtime involves a leg stretch in Battersea Park and some indulgence in his favourite obsession, tennis balls – but only the yellow variety. This is then followed by another snooze to recharge the batteries.

Days off are truly golden. Greenwich Park sells bacon butties and hot coffee and freely supplies large numbers of squirrels for chasing. Sometimes they also include getting extremely wet as Charlie often forgets to look in front of him when running towards the boating lake.

Warm summer afternoons are spent exploring London, ambling through Soho, flirting with tourists and café staff and generally enjoying the simple pleasures in life.

Alfie & Oscar

Alfie and Oscar, the double trouble Westie duo, work in the fundraising department with Fiona.

She is Battersea's Westie aficionado and it seemed only natural for the vet to present her with the little bundle of gorgeousness otherwise know as Alfie the Peacemaker.

Found wandering the streets of Putney, Alfie was suffering from 'lion jaw', a very painful condition where one side of the jaw grows quicker than the other.

Oscar had been given in by a family because he had behavioural problems. He was frightened, aggressive, hyperactive and neurotic with a pathological hatred of mountain bikes. Another great dog for Fiona! Under Alfie's guidance Oscar learnt how to play, deal with his fear and aggression issues and even discover the joy of swimming.

Their working day is incredibly full, beginning with a cacophony of barking when the post bag arrives. Then, possibly the most important task of the day is the reminder for the mid-morning sausage breakfast run. The staff could waste away without their prompting. At any given moment they also like to throw in a five-minute mayhem session that keeps everyone in their chairs or pressed against the wall. They inspect and greet all new visitors and regularly attend meetings of interest.

On a serious note they are actively involved in the foster mentoring scheme and whenever Fiona brings another dog home they help resolve its issues and get it ready for a brand new life.